THE AGILE CONCEPT

For business and Personal growth

agility requires a change in thinking and a willingness to let go of outdated beliefs and practices.

I hope the Agile Business and Personal Development Philosophy inspires you to explore new possibilities, change and embark on a journey of continuous learning and improvement.   I would like to thank numerous people who contributed to the development of the Agile concept. Their views, experiences and stories support this book and provide insight into the transformative power of agility. Finally, I would like to thank my readers for joining me on this journey of transformation. I believe the insights and tools shared on these pages will allow you to quickly understand and unlock your full potential in business and life. Let this book be your driving force for growth, innovation and success as you navigate today's changing world.   We recommend that you change the reading.

Best Regards,
Ajay Kumar

Agile development

Agile methodologies were born in the 1990s due to the limitations of traditional linear project management methods. The planning, development, testing, and deployment phases have been streamlined in the popular waterfall paradigm, often leading to delays, inefficiencies, and loss of capacity to innovate. Agile was developed out of a need for a more flexible and iterative methodology.

The Agile Manifesto

In 2001, a group of software development experts came together and drafted the Agile Manifesto. This foundational document outlined a set of guiding principles for Agile development. The manifesto emphasizes individuals and interactions over processes and tools, working software over comprehensive documentation, customer collaboration over contract negotiation, and responding to change over following a plan.

The Agile Manifesto highlights the value of adaptability, continuous improvement, and customer-centricity. It encourages teams to embrace change, prioritize collaboration and communication, and focus on delivering tangible results. The principles of the Agile Manifesto were originally conceived for software development and have proven applicable and innovative beyond the realm of coding.

Implementing Agile

Principles Agile is not limited to software development. Its principles apply to all areas of life. Flexible living is about using flexible thinking and flexible practices to deal with the complexities and uncertainties of today's world. The foundation of an agile life is to see change as an immutable and inevitable part of life. Agile encourages us to see change as an opportunity to grow and improve rather than resist it. By adopting a growth mind-set and remaining open to new opportunities, we are better able to adapt and thrive in a dynamic environment. A flexible lifestyle means continuous improvement. We encourage people to set goals, take action, and learn from experiences. Iterations and feedback loops play an important role in this process, allowing ideas to take shape and goals to be achieved incrementally. Another important aspect of flexible living is adaptability and flexibility. Agile encourages us to be flexible in our plans and processes, ready to adapt and adapt to changing circumstances. By developing resilience and the ability to meet unexpected challenges, we can navigate uncertainty with confidence. Agile living also promotes self-organization and empowerment. It recognizes the importance of freedom and responsibility to enable individuals and groups to make decisions, manage their business and move forward. Collaboration and effective communication play a key role in promoting teamwork and intelligence. In the next chapter, we'll look at these quick applications and how they can apply to different areas of life. From personal and social development to health and wellness, Agile principles are useful and practical to help you live a more productive life again. When we start living the good life, remember that holding the heart doesn't mean succeeding or surviving all difficulties. Instead, it is about harmonizing, embracing change, and constantly learning and adapting. By applying these principles to your daily life, you can create purpose, balance, and success in a rapidly changing world.

Part I

Agile Mind-set

thinking is a philosophy that emphasizes flexibility, customer focus and iterative development. It started in software development, but has since spread its influence to other areas. An agile strategy empowers people to embrace change, value collaboration, and focus on delivering customer value in a timely manner.

Fundamentals of Agile Thinking

Embracing Change: Agile thinking encourages people to see change as an opportunity for growth and development, rather than resisting it. Agile practitioners understand that change is inevitable and that rapid change can lead to better results.

Customer engagement: Agile teams value customer feedback and collaboration throughout the development process. We work closely with our customers to get information that helps us improve and improve our products or services to meet people's needs.

Iterative development: Agile teams divide their projects into small, manageable milestones called iterations or sprints. This iteration allows for frequent feedback, learning, and class revision. By submitting additional work early and often, the team can tweak and revise the work based on the feedback received.

Team Empowerment: Agile values the importance of self-managing and cohesive teams. This group is independent and has the right to run its own business. Organizations can unleash the potential of their teams by fostering a culture of trust and collaboration. Continuing Education: Specialists receive continuing education and professional development. They regularly review processes, celebrate successes, and identify areas for growth. This learning culture enables teams to adapt and respond effectively to new challenges and opportunities.

Advantages of flexible thinking: adaptability. Agile thinking enables people and organizations to respond quickly to changing circumstances. A change-ready team can quickly adjust strategies, priorities, and plans and stay ahead in a rapidly changing environment.

Developing Collaboration: Agile thinking fosters a culture of collaboration, trust, and open communication. By working effectively together, teams can leverage the different skills and perspectives of their members, resulting in better problem solving and innovation.

Customer satisfaction: Agile teams gain insight and feedback by engaging customers in the development process. This customer-oriented approach ensures customer satisfaction by ensuring that the final product or service is close to the customer's needs and expectations.

Faster time-to-market: The nature of Agile enables teams to deliver incremental projects quickly. This allows organizations to bring key features and functionality to the market first, gain a competitive advantage and shorten time to market. quality improvement. Continuous learning and frequent feedback during rapid development can improve quality. By incorporating feedback into every iteration, teams can improve performance by identifying and fixing issues in a timely manner.

The Benefits of Agile Thinking

Adaptability: Agile thinking enables people and organizations to respond quickly to changing situations. Teams that embrace change can quickly adjust their strategies, priorities, and plans and keep them ahead in a fast-paced environment. Developing

Collaboration: Agile thinking fosters a culture of collaboration, trust, and open communication. By working effectively together, teams can leverage the different skills and perspectives of their members, resulting in better problem solving and innovation.

Customer Satisfaction: Agile teams gain insight and feedback by engaging customers in the development process. This customer-oriented approach ensures customer satisfaction by ensuring that the final product or service is close to the customer's needs and expectations.

Reduce time-to-market: The nature of Agile allows teams to deliver incremental projects quickly. This enables organizations to be the first to market with key capabilities, gain a competitive advantage and accelerate time-to-market.

Quality improvement: Continuous learning and frequent feedback during rapid development can improve quality. By incorporating feedback into every iteration, the team can identify and address issues in a timely manner, resulting in improved performance.

Part II

Agile practices

Practices have revolutionized project management and product development, giving organizations flexibility and efficiency to solve complex problems. According to the Agile Manifesto, these practices are essential for collaboration, exchange and customer value. In this article, we'll explore some agile practices and their benefits, focusing on how they increase productivity and foster innovation in teams and organizations.

User Stories and Product Backlog: User Stories is an agile application focused on capturing user needs and wants. Short, customer-focused instructions focus on a specific description or function from the user's perspective. Stories use teams to better understand user expectations and guide improvement. These are organized and prioritized in the Product Backlog, a dynamic product list that represents the products needed. This practice ensures that the relationship with the customer needs to be improved and allows the team to make informed decisions about what to build next.

Iterative and Incremental Development: Agile practices encourage iterative and incremental development to deliver value early and often. Instead of the traditional waterfall process of putting all requirements together first, agile teams break the work into smaller iterations or sprints. Each iteration results in more work being done on the product. This approach allows the team to collect feedback from stakeholders and end users throughout the development process, allowing them to improve and develop the product. Iterative and incremental development reduces the risk of late failure, increases customer satisfaction, and provides time for course correction.

Daily Talks: Also known as Daily Meetings, Daily Talks are short meetings where partners provide updates and discuss issues or issues. These meetings promote collaboration, transparency and accountability among teams. By sharing information and solving problems in a timely manner, stand-up meetings encourage collaboration and teamwork. They allow the team to identify and resolve barriers, provide effective communication and provide overall project visibility.

Continuous Integration and Testing: Continuous Integration and Testing is an important aspect of agile work that emphasizes continuous integration of code changes and continuous testing. Rather than waiting until the end of the development cycle to collaborate and test, agile teams collaborate and test their code frequently, often several times a day. This approach enables early detection of defects, improves policy quality, and reduces the risk of integration issues. Continuous integration and testing to ensure that the team provides stable products, the quality of products is increased, and the whole process is improved.

Retrospectives and Continuous Improvement: Retrospectives are regular meetings where teams reflect on their work and identify areas for improvement. This rapid implementation fosters a culture of continuous learning and allows teams to adapt and improve their processes. When they return, members discuss what went well, what could be improved, and make suggestions for future iterations. By constantly thinking about performance, agile teams can identify conflicts, improve business processes, and implement changes that increase productivity and productivity.

Benefits of Agile Practices:

Shortened time-to-market: Agile practices enable teams to deliver valuable products early and frequently. This fast turnaround time shortens time to market, enabling organizations to quickly respond to changing customer needs and gain competitive advantage.

Ensuring customer satisfaction: Agile practices involve customers in the development process and prioritize their needs, ensuring that the final product is of high quality in line with customer needs. This customer-oriented approach ensures customer satisfaction and loyalty.

Improve Collaboration and Communication: Agile practices support collaboration, transparency, and effective team communication. Daily challenges, user stories, and feedback help build a culture of collaboration, break down silos, and expand collaboration.

flexibility and adaptability: An agile approach gives you the flexibility to respond to changes and priorities. Iterative step-by-step development with continuous feedback allows teams to adapt their work to changing conditions so that the final product meets the needs of the current business.

Continuous learning and innovation: Agile practitioners encourage a culture of continuous learning, improvement and innovation. Retrospectives provide a platform for teams to reflect on their business, identify areas for growth, and test new ideas. This creates an environment where creativity and innovation thrive.

Conclusion: Agile methods have proven effective for project management and production. Agile development practices emphasize user eccentricity, collaboration, and iterative development that enable organizations to be efficient, productive, and innovative. These applications enable teams to respond effectively to change, reduce time-to-market and increase customer satisfaction. By adopting agile practices, organizations can thrive in today's rapidly changing and competitive business environment.

Part III

Applying Agile in Different Areas of Life

Originally developed for software development, agile methods are gaining popularity in many industries because they can effectively manage complex projects. However, the principle of exchange, cooperation, and exchange can be out of place in the workplace. Flexibility in many areas of life enables people and organizations to deal with uncertainty, embrace change, and more. In this article, we'll look at how Agile can be used for personal development, education, project management, and business.

Personal growth with Agile

Applying agile principles to personal growth can be a powerful tool for advancement and rejuvenation as people deal with life's challenges. Agile methods were developed for software development, emphasizing flexibility, collaboration, and iterative learning. In this article, we'll explore how agility can be used for personal growth, enabling people to embrace change, overcome challenges and reach their potential.

Setting Clear Goals and Further Learning: Agile methodologies encourage setting clear and attainable goals, a method that can be used directly for personal growth. Individuals can create opportunities for their personal development by setting specific and measurable goals. However, flexible thinking recognizes that goals may change or evolve over time. People should view their goals as emotions to be tested and developed through repeated learning.

Break down goals into manageable tasks: Agile breaks large projects into smaller, more manageable tasks. Likewise, personal growth can be achieved by breaking down long-term goals into small, actionable steps. Breaking down your goals into something achievable helps people stay focused, track their progress, and increase their motivation. This approach ensures that personal development remains visible and achievable, avoids stress, and promotes a sense of accomplishment.

Regular feedback and self-evaluation : Agile processes emphasize the importance of frequent feedback. Likewise, regular self-assessment and feedback contributes to personal growth. People should create opportunities to reflect on their achievements, identify areas for improvement, and celebrate their successes. Honest self-assessment allows people to adjust their strategies and make necessary adjustments to their goals.

Embrace change and learn from failure : Agile encourages people to embrace change and see it as an opportunity for growth. Setbacks and setbacks are unavoidable in personal development, but should be viewed as valuable learning opportunities. Using awareness, people can change their thinking to see failure as an opportunity for growth and improvement. Accepting change and learning from failure allows people to adapt to their own ways and explore new possibilities.

Testing and continuous improvement: Agile methods
support testing and continuous improvement. Likewise,
personal growth requires people to step out of their comfort
zone, try new things, and learn from results. By trying
different methods, people can decide which method works
best for them and make an informed decision for personal
growth. Encouraging continuous improvement encourages
people to continue developing and developing new skills and
ideas.

Co-operation and support : Personal growth is a personal
journey, but the cooperation and support of others can
contribute to a successful career. Agile principles emphasize
the importance of collaboration and effective
communication. Seeking support from a mentor, coach, or
like-minded person can provide validation, accountability,
and support as you personally evolve. Collaboration
promotes learning, broadens horizons, and fosters personal
growth.

Agile in education

Education plays an important role in equipping people with
the knowledge and skills they need to thrive in a changing
world. Adopting agile concepts in education can transform
the learning process, as traditional education systems often
struggle to keep up with rapid changes. Agile methods have
been developed for software development that emphasize
flexibility.

Flexibility in Course Design: Agile methodologies help to plan flexibly and respond to change. Likewise, curricula in education are flexible enough to create Customization. Using agile methods such as Scrum or Kanban, teachers can create lessons that adapt to individual learning, interests, and pace. This flexibility improves their overall learning by allowing students to interact with information in a resonant way.

Iterative Learning and Continuous Feedback: Agile encourages iterative learning and continuous improvement through frequent feedback. In science education, this instruction can be implemented through continuous assessment and feedback strategies. By giving students immediate feedback on their performance, teachers can identify areas for improvement and adjust their teaching strategies accordingly. Retrospective learning enables students to track their learning, make necessary adjustments, and ultimately achieve better learning outcomes.

Collaborative and Student-Centric Approaches: Agile methods encourage collaboration and teamwork, and these principles can be used effectively in the classroom. Create a student environment that encourages participation, engagement and positive thinking. Agility-inspired practices such as teamwork, peer learning and collaborative problem solving develop communication and operational skills. Students learn to work together, leverage each other's strengths, and develop interpersonal skills critical to success in today's world.

Agile Tools and Techniques: Agile methodologies come with many tools and techniques that can be used in learning. Agile

Kanban boards like Kanban can help teachers see and manage learning and progress. This tool provides transparent communication and collaboration between teachers and students. Additionally, rigorous practices such as user stories and feedback can be used to gather feedback from students, identify areas for improvement, and continue to improve the learning process.

Embrace Technology and Blended Learning: Agile methodologies see technology as enabling and collaborative. Technology can be used in education to promote blended learning. Online platforms, learning management systems, and interactive digital resources can facilitate self-learning, provide instant feedback, and enable asynchronous collaboration. Blended learning models that combine online and offline activities support flexibility, accessibility and flexibility of learning.

Adapt to changing requirements : Agile processes are known for their ability to adapt to change and changing requirements. By following simple rules, teachers can adapt to business needs, technological developments, and social changes. This includes relevant content, curriculum updates, and providing students with the knowledge and skills they need to succeed in a rapidly changing world.

Agile in Project management

Project management is changing rapidly, now people needs new ideas and new mind-set. Conversely, Agile methodologies have gained significant traction due to their ability to promote agility, collaboration, and adaptability. Originally developed for software development, agile principles can be applied across industries to improve project outcomes. This article explores how agile methodologies can transform project management by facilitating iterative delivery, enhancing collaboration, and enabling rapid adaptation to changing requirements.

Iterative and incremental offers: One of the core principles of agile project management is the concept of iterative and incremental implementation. Instead of waiting for the entire project to be completed, Agile breaks projects into smaller, manageable increments called "sprints." Each sprint focuses on delivering a valuable subset of the project's objectives. This iterative approach allows for continuous feedback, encourages early customer involvement, and enables the project team to adapt and refine their work based on stakeholder input. The result is a more flexible and responsive project delivery process.

Embracing Change: Unlike traditional project management methodologies that resist changes once the project plan is established, Agile embraces change as a natural part of the project lifecycle. Agile teams are encouraged to be flexible and adapt to evolving requirements. Changes can be incorporated seamlessly during the project through ongoing collaboration with stakeholders. This adaptability ensures that project outcomes align with stakeholder expectations, even in the face of shifting priorities or market conditions.

Transparent Communication and Collaboration: Agile project management emphasizes frequent and transparent communication among team members and stakeholders. Daily stand-up meetings, regular progress updates, and continuous collaboration enable effective coordination and alignment within the project team. This level of transparency promotes better decision-making, encourages shared ownership, and facilitates the early identification of potential issues or bottlenecks. Agile teams collaborate independently and use the diverse skills and perspectives of all team members.

Empowerment of the project team: Agile methodologies empower project teams by fostering a culture of trust, autonomy, and self-organization. The project team is jointly responsible for the success of the project and is responsible for making decisions to achieve the desired outcome. This autonomy allows team members to be more creative, innovative, and engaged in their work. Agile project management enables project teams to increase motivation, productivity, and overall project productivity.

Continuous Improvement and Feedback: Agile project management encourages continuous improvement through regular retrospectives. After each sprint or project phase, the team reflects on what went well, identifies areas for improvement, and determines actionable steps to enhance future performance. This feedback loop ensures that lessons learned are captured and applied iteratively throughout the project. Continuous improvement enhances project outcomes, optimizes processes, and enables the team to adapt and grow over time.

Adapting Tools and Techniques: Agile methodologies come with a wide array of tools and techniques that support effective project management. An Agile board, such as a Kanban or Scrum board, provides a visual representation of a project's goals, progress, and priorities. These tools help teams stay organized, track progress, and effectively manage workflow. Agile project management improves overall performance and team productivity.

Agile in Entrepreneurship

Entrepreneurship is a dynamic and often unpredictable practice that requires flexibility, patience and a refusal to innovate. In this rapidly changing environment, traditional business practices may not be able to keep up. Known for its simplicity and collaboration, agile methodologies have become a solid foundation for business success. This article explores how businesses can use agile concepts to drive innovation, overcome uncertainty, and spur business growth.

Acceptance of uncertainty: Its essence lies in uncertainty. Agile methodologies give entrepreneurs the will to achieve productive results and deal with uncertainty. Rather than trying to predict and manage every change, agile entrepreneurs recognize that the future is unpredictable and focus on building resilience and resilience. By stepping back on product development and business recognition, entrepreneurs can gather feedback, make informed decisions, and adjust strategies as needed.

Minimum Viable Product (MVP) and Iterative Development: The concept of Minimum Viable Product (MVP) is closely aligned with Agile principles. Agile entrepreneurs focus on providing a minimum number of processes that add value to the target business, rather than dedicating huge resources to creating a high-performing product. This iterative development allows marketers to test their ideas, collect user feedback, and improve their products based on actual use. Entrepreneurs can quickly analyze their business strategy, reduce risk and make informed decisions using the MVP strategy.

Continuous Innovation and Feedback: Agile methodologies emphasize the importance of continuous learning and improvement. In business, this means a constant pursuit of innovation and a culture of experimentation. Agile entrepreneurs actively seek input from customers, stakeholders and business experts to gather insights and identify new opportunities. By integrating feedback into the process, marketers can identify pain points, meet customer needs, and improve their products and models.

Quick Adaptation and Market Sensitivity: In today's business environment, the ability to adapt quickly to changes in the market is essential. Agile methods provide entrepreneurs with the tools to quickly respond to new trends, customer needs and competitive pressure. Marketers can monitor the market regularly, stay in touch with customers, and use analytics to adjust strategies in real time. Agile entrepreneurs aren't afraid to change business models, iterate on products, or explore new business opportunities.

Collaboration and cross-functional work: Agile methods are more important than collaboration and cross-functional work. Bringing more people and technology together in business processes is critical. Agile entrepreneurs create environments where partners collaborate, share ideas, and encourage collaboration. This partnership can provide a broader perspective, encourage creativity, and create a sense of ownership and commitment to the business.

Agile Project Management and Lean Start-up: Agile project management frameworks such as Scrum or Kanban complete the business journey. This process organizes, prioritizes, and tracks tasks for completion, providing structure and simplifying project execution. Additionally, integrating Lean Start-up principles with Agile methodologies enables entrepreneurs to optimize resources, reduce waste, and accelerate time-to-market.

Agile with Lean principles

The combination of Agile and Lean concepts has proven to be a powerful force in the world of business and project management. Agile processes provide flexibility, adaptability and continuous improvement, while eliminating waste, optimizing processes and delivering value are the core principles. When these two perspectives are integrated, organizations can achieve greater productivity, efficiency and customer satisfaction. In this article, we'll explore how Agile and Lean work together and how their integration can change the way we work.

Agile: Flexibility, Collaboration, and Iterative Development Agile methods such as Scrum and Kanban encourage flexibility, collaboration, and iterative development. Teams have short work cycles and often offer little extra value. Agile teams continue to improve their product or service by accepting change and incorporating feedback, enabling customers and stakeholders to meet changes.

Lean: Eliminate Waste and Create Value Derived from the Toyota Production System, Lean principles focus on eliminating waste and creating value for customers. Waste comes in many forms, including overproduction, excess inventory, defects, unnecessary work and waiting time. Lean methodologies such as Lean Six Sigma aim to improve processes, reduce waste and improve quality. Lean helps organizations successfully deliver products or services by mapping value streams and identifying areas for improvement. Agile and Lean Complements The combination of Agile and Lean creates synergies that can increase operational efficiency. Agile methods provide the basis for iterative development, while lean principles guide the process of continuous improvement. Together, they make the team efficient and customer-focused. Agile's focus on collaboration and change complements Lean's focus on reducing waste and creating value. Agile enables teams to respond quickly to change and increase costs, while Lean ensures process efficiency, zero waste, and customer satisfaction. Continuous improvement and Kaizen Agile and Lean emphasize continuous improvement. In lean manufacturing, this principle is called Kaizen and encourages small changes to move forward. Agile methodologies embody this concept through regular feedback and feedback, where teams reflect on their performance, identify areas for improvement, and implement changes in the next iteration. By combining agility with lean, organizations can create a culture of continuous improvement that leads to innovation, performance and growth. Value Stream Mapping and Process

Optimization Value Stream Mapping is one of the powerful tools that can be combined with Agile in Lean. A value stream diagram shows visibility and analysis of the end-to-end process from initial demand to final delivery of the product or service. By identifying inconsistencies, duplication, and non-value-added steps, teams can improve processes and eliminate waste. Agile teams can use the value stream to identify areas where the development backlog can be improved and optimized. By applying lean principles, agile teams can reduce cycle time, increase productivity, and deliver better results.

Conclusion: The integration of Agile and Lean principles is a way to maximize efficiency, effectiveness and customer satisfaction. Agile processes bring flexibility, collaboration, and iterative improvements, while principles eliminate waste and optimize processes. Organizations that recognize the success of Agile and Lean can create a culture of continuous improvement, foster innovation and achieve operational excellence. The combination of Agile and Lean enables teams to respond quickly to change, deliver more value, and improve processes for greater efficiency. This integration enables organizations to remain competitive, adapt to customer needs and drive long-term growth. By using the agile power of Lean principles, organizations can reach their potential and be successful in today's business world and competition.

Summarize

The agile philosophy has become a fundamental shift on the foundation of software development. The principles of adaptation, collaboration and change have been applied in many areas, including business and personal development. Agile methodologies help businesses embrace change, prioritize customer satisfaction, facilitate continuous learning, and encourage transparent communication. At the same time, people can use simple principles to set goals, accept change and failure, seek cooperation and feedback, and improve regularly. This article explores the power of Agile to transform business processes and foster personal growth and unlock their potential for success and growth.

Agile methodologies have transformed businesses by providing flexibility and the ability to manage projects, respond to customer needs, and drive innovation.

The Agile philosophy is not limited to business, but provides an important foundation for personal growth and development. Agile principles enable people to deal with uncertainty, embrace change, and continuously improve.

The agile philosophy transforms business and personal development by promoting flexibility, collaboration and flexibility. Agile processes in business enable organizations to embrace change, prioritize customer satisfaction, facilitate continuous learning, streamline communication and empower teams. Agile principles drive innovation, increase productivity, and help businesses succeed in today's business environment. At the individual level, agile principles encourage personal growth by promoting purpose, fostering change and failure, seeking collaboration and feedback, and finding solutions. The agile philosophy encourages people to overcome challenges, embrace uncertainty and achieve personal growth. By embracing the power of agility, businesses and individuals can unlock their full potential and succeed in their careers.

The end